Waiting for Tomorrow

Waiting for Tomorrow

A Poetry Collection

THOMAS JUAREZ

RESOURCE *Publications* • Eugene, Oregon

WAITING FOR TOMORROW
A Poetry Collection

Copyright © 2025 Thomas Juarez. All rights reserved. Except for brief quotations in critical publications or reviews, no part of this book may be reproduced in any manner without prior written permission from the publisher. Write: Permissions, Wipf and Stock Publishers, 199 W. 8th Ave., Suite 3, Eugene, OR 97401.

Resource Publications
An Imprint of Wipf and Stock Publishers
199 W. 8th Ave., Suite 3
Eugene, OR 97401

www.wipfandstock.com

PAPERBACK ISBN: 979-8-3852-5274-9
HARDCOVER ISBN: 979-8-3852-5275-6
EBOOK ISBN: 979-8-3852-5276-3
VERSION NUMBER 05/29/25

For Makenna and Beau, with love.

Contents

Acknowledgments	ix
Introduction	xi
Tears of Rain	1
Fairy Ring	3
Circle at Midnight	4
Grey Hat	6
As I Sleep	7
Words	8
Abstraction	9
Happy	10
Fortnight	11
Why	12
Enigma	13
Teardrop	15
Sun Four	17
Storyteller	19
Circle of Life	21
Forgiveness	22
So Long	23
Life, Love, Happiness	24
Lucidity in Dream	25
Kiss of Tea	27
Coming Home	28
Louie	30

Contents

Trinkets and Doodads	32
Country Girl	33
Faded Dreams	34
The End is Nigh	36
The Old Man and the Tree	37
Modern Dragon Slayers	38
Dark Matter of Time	39
Waiting for Tomorrow	41
Storm	42
I Forgot You	43
Silver Bullet	45
Studio	47
When I Think of Oklahoma	48
Voodoo Doll	49
Wants and Dreams	50
See Me	52
Here Comes Another	54
Myriad Botanical Gardens (OKC)	56
Dark Bites	57
Behind Enemy Lines	59
Addiction Analysis	61
Insomnia	63
27	66
Brown Headed Blackbirds	67
Rebirth of the American (Bison)	68
Seasonal	69
Finding Myself	70
I Miss My Army Friends	71
Sovereignty	72
Trigger Warning	73
Dedication	74
Crisis Line	75
About a Few of These Poems	77

Acknowledgments

I am grateful to the University of Central Oklahoma for publishing two of these poems (Happy and Abstraction) in their spring 2024 publication.

I am also grateful to Cameron University in Lawton, Oklahoma (for so many things).

A special thank you to my wife, Lucinda Juarez (for absolutely everything).

Introduction

About half of these poems were written in a notebook I named "The Book of Nonsense"—a book that I filled with 72 hand-written poems in 8 days. A further 20% of this collection came from the notebook that followed "The Book of Nonsense" (that took a week or two longer but was 80 pages front and back). I completed the collection by adding in some poems that'd been sitting around waiting for edits and sprinkling in a few new, unrelated poems.

The title of this collection comes from my ponderings about the concept of tomorrow as well as life, love, family, and dreams. I have tried to pour as much "me" as I could into as many poems as I could (keeping in mind that some are more conceptual than they are literal or practical).

TEARS OF RAIN

Standing alone on the back porch, trying to tune in to my emotions, I watch the sun fade as it comes to rest peacefully behind a pleasant and perfect horizon. You were born a few short hours ago, you see, and I've come outside to look for a sign.

As night continues to darken, I look skyward, thinking the sign might meet, then greet me, somewhere in the middle—somewhere between the kings and queens of the celestial jungle, somewhere where north, south, east, and west are as meaningless as yesterday—somewhere where tomorrow is real.

Please understand dearest child, it is not ritual nor is it tradition that calls me outdoors on the night of your birth, though I do find myself wishing wayward ships of tradition would return to our shores and grant me a sign. A sign to tell me why such a bright light was sent to help us recover from the pandemic that plagues us:

a single, floating, yellowish-white light descends from the east. I can nearly touch it, though I dare not move a muscle because I know what it is. It is but one of what used to be hundreds. A creature coveted by the children of my time.

Fireflies once floated on air,
I swear, it's true, dearest girl.

Tears of rain flood the plains,
from my heart to you
when I think of heaven's
miracles you may never see.

TEARS OF RAIN

Tears of rain, dearest child,
may you always feel loved.

I leave you with a secret:

Many years ago, when I was a child, the fireflies would dance in the air amongst us and light fires of goodness in our eyes. Our delicately freckled faces would watch, in wonder, for only the briefest of moments. You see, we believed the fireflies came to play with us, and there was little time to waste. In our haste, we forgot to enjoy their beauty. We never imagined a day when such wonders would join the ships of old and leave us. But today—in this moment, by the light of a dream, a sign was delivered. I know it, and I don't know why—I just do.

Tears of rain, sweetest girl,
now reach for the sky.
Tears of rain as I cry,
and fireflies light the night.

FAIRY RING

I planted a garden for you, beautiful child,

It wasn't for joy of playing in dirt.
Not for flowers, trees, nor bushes.

It wasn't for fairies, gnomes, toadstools,
or multi-colored solar mushroom lights—
it was out of love for you.

I wanted you to see pretty pebbles,
Gerber daisies, and butterfly bushes.

I wanted to see you run toward roses,
then turn and dash toward salvias,
and I wanted you to smell sagebrush
when the sun sets over Sterling.

I wanted you to see the magical
and the mystical, and I always want
you to remember that we love you—
our brave, beautiful child.

CIRCLE AT MIDNIGHT

A gnome and a mushroom fairy house
    are set in an outer circle
of rounded pebbles, guarding the easternmost
    and southernmost entrances
to an inner circle. Northernmost and westernmost
    entrances are guarded
only by illusionary discs of confusion, and stone.

For weeks, I have been clearing away
    winter rubble while,
at the very same time, deliberately keeping
    my feet outside the inside circle,
where magic resides.

The statue of a silly clay frog looks on—
    I stare back, intently.

Tonight brings first full moon of spring—
    brush and daisy will wake,
buds will form flowers, and the ancient ones
    will return. On the twelfth
midnight stroke, we turn our hats about and run
    around the outer circle nine times—
not one step more.

CIRCLE AT MIDNIGHT

The sunwise direction of our trot will entice
    little winged ladies to return,
our backwards hats will show we mean no harm,
    and gentle giggles of children will
welcome equally gentle fairies back to their home—
    back here, with us.

Tonight, we celebrate magic.

GREY HAT

I Couldn't find my hat.

I looked high, I looked low,
I looked both here and there,
I couldn't find that hat anywhere.

It's as grey as it is plain,
or rather, it's plainly grey.
I like to wear my hat when it's time to play.

I searched high and low one last time,
and of this time, whatever did I find?

The sweetest girl my heart has known,
playing with my old hat, she now owns.

AS I SLEEP

she tells me,
while i sleep,
that she still loves me.

she tells me,
while i sleep,
that she still cares.

she tells me through lips
sweet like honey—
and she sews wildflowers through her hair.

and she still believes she can be happy.
and she still feels bereft of air.

she tells me.

she loves me.

as i pretend to sleep.

WORDS

i used to think
i was broken.
i wasn't.

wounds softened,
wounds healed,
because of you—

because i admired you,
and because—
because you were you.

but that's all over now.

all over but the crying,
all over but the hiding,
all over but—

all over but the wounds,
left on you, by me—
left on me, by you—

words are worthless.

ABSTRACTION

Imagine a single bite of chocolate—

it's as soft as it is creamy,
like a little piece of heaven.

Now Imagine the breeze blowing through your hair—

a catamaran ride into powdery-blue horizons,
and the breath that you've stolen from its bow.

Or maybe it's a soft summer morning—

and the shadow of the moon is still in sight.
You feel your heart beat, anticipating sunrise.

***

As for me, I can imagine nearly anything.

All day long I think of days gone by.
I imagine what it might be like to be happy—

I imagine, then I cry.

HAPPY

I couldn't be happier if I tried—
really.

Spring has sprung and my world is alive:
roses—
daisies—
and petunias hanging by the door.

Gloved fingers sifting through black soil,
cup—
scoop—
gently set the new flower in place.

Bidding red and dotted ladies good day,
coreopsis—
cosmos—
whatever I can plant to make them stay.

Working with the sun on my back.

Playing, like a child, in the rain.

I feel I've come to life again.

Really—
I couldn't be happier if I tried.

FORTNIGHT

Fourteen days.
Fourteen ways,
to say I love you.

When I wake and see you, my heart flutters and smiles.
When a falling teardrop lands on my pillowtop.
When the weight of love is lost on words.
When I say forever.
When my feet float on air.
When my voice crackles as I say I care.
When I hold your hand.
When I squeeze it.
When I plant spring flowers; every one of them, for you.
When I kiss the air.
When it kisses back.
When I tell you I need you.
When the world goes dark—and I pull you close.
When I dream the sweetest dreams of you.

You see—
I do love you,
every single day.

WHY

because sun kisses moon / and you / because today/ I found love / in you / because stars shimmer brightly / above you / because stars brought me to you / because love is the gift we chase after / because love is the joy we have found / because love / is.

ENIGMA

your face—
once freckled with emotion,
now riddled with fine lines—
chock-full of lies.

for years,
i thought you treated
me as harshly
as the world treated you.

then,
as your lips pouted
i remembered
red.

your lips, so red.
so lush and warm.
saturated with sweetness.
full of promise.

but—no more.

years battling loneliness
have left your lips dry,
cracked, and withered.
so, i search your eyes.

those eyes—unbending,
they see past everything,
everything fallible,
everything me.

scanning and searching
they find nothing but grey matter,
so they narrow their gaze—

they squeeze, then squint,
squeeze, then squint—
until they find someone.

someone fervent.
someone forgiving.
someone new.

TEARDROP

My hand—
my arm, my face, my . . .
whatever you want,
whenever you want,
if you can and if you will,
please—
touch me?

The palm of your hand,
in or out of mine,
at any given time—
is welcome.

If you could nudge my elbow
or run your dry fingers
across my expressionless face,
if you could but look away,
toward a warm, distant place—
where your hand still fits in mine.

Oh, what I wouldn't give for one more touch.
What I wouldn't give—
I miss you so much.

And I promise not to push you so far away.
And I promise that from this day forward,
I will not wander to lands beyond reach.

TEARDROP

But if I might ask a small favor,
as I hope to savor
the moment your skin touches mine:
touch me,
whenever and wherever you please,
but do not wipe the teardrop from my eye—
I cried it just for you.

Touch me?

SUN FOUR

rain—
catches ride on wind,
harnesses
vital, raw energy—
unleashes
maelstrom
powered by rage,
remorse,
and regret.

waters washed in by currents
washed me out,
and washed me away—

until i arrived here,

and a father figure
found me—
spoke to me.

happens
he said,
when we turn from the sun.

*happens
when we run from the sun,*
he said.

SUN FOUR

he smiled, he turned,
he blindly walked away,

after 52 years of rain.

STORYTELLER

I forgot the way you moved—

tiptoeing around the world,
imagining invisible floorboards
shuffling beneath you, and you
glide right over them, dipping
your toes into hidden clouds.

But the first time your feet froze,
you panicked. You said it was like
being suffocated—like drowning
in a river of stale, stagnant air.

But some clouds get even thicker,
you said—even heavier than others.
And all clouds must cry. So, that's
what you did, you found courage
and you cried—then you ran.

Until the next time your feet
froze—and it was even worse.
Second cloud spawned six
eyes, so you ran. You just
clenched your fists and you ran.

Ten down, I heard you say life
was meant to be a very grand,
very opulent prize. And love?

Love should be soft—
warm.

But time will come again,
Fae,
and your walls will narrow.

Whatever you do, Fae,
don't you stop.

Don't stop running, Fae.

Don't stop.

CIRCLE OF LIFE

after time
        sun splits—
                still, light.

motionless
        masses of water—
                ceased currents.

life remains,
        though fractured,
                life remains.

north needle
        orients east,
                life . . . remains.

FORGIVENESS

I'm still holding on,
waiting to see if
forgiveness finds you.

I've heard you, time
and again, wondering
aloud why others refuse
to see past your shortcomings.

Wondering if, maybe, in some
small way, they could see fit
to forgive you—
how happy you could be.

I want that too—
from you.

I hurt you,
I was wrong,

I could not help myself from—
well, you know.

Read this or not,
forgive me or not,
please find peace.

SO LONG

Love was lost on a Monday morning.

The sky was clear,
the wind, hollow.
I didn't see it coming.

She left her diary beside
the bed along with a note,
instructing me to read it.

Feeling no need for such nonsense,
I pitched the pages into my fireplace.

Pages soaked with gasoline.
Gasoline lit by match.

As memories burned,
I fed the dog breakfast.

He was always the better friend anyway.

LIFE, LOVE, HAPPINESS

The smell of soft-wooded sagebrush—

The sight of raindrops lightly tapping treetops—

The thought of roses flirting with honeybees—

The sun shining through my easternmost window in the west—

Life—

Love—

Happiness—

If this is a dream,
do not wake me.

LUCIDITY IN DREAM

dreams spill into being,
not touchable,
nearly visible—
surging.

i cannot see them,
but i can feel them;
and i feel me—
riding,

tunneling through the surge,
becoming drunk on power—
drunk on time.
lost.

so, i ran.

i ran to solid ground,
finding lost pieces of myself
and gathering them in the sand,
like shells on a beach.

each shell has its own story,
each its own embrace, its own
mercy. and in my favorite shell,
the only thing i see is you.

LUCIDITY IN DREAM

i like to imagine you'll wrap
a scarf around your face—
i'd say i love you,
and you would smile.

i could see it in your eyes.
you would smile—

and i would lie there, lucidly,
in dream.

KISS OF TEA

I gathered dried leaves of maple, pecan, walnut, and elm in droves just before the bitter cold of last week's arctic blast. During the bitter cold, I dared not step my aging body into the hornet's nest of icicles outside my door. Outside my door it was cold, wet, and wonderful—but not for me. For me, I have a home I made with you to keep us warm when nature's beauty bites. It bites but a few days a year in our earthly plot of land granted us by heavenly grace. For if heaven's grace were truly here, what else could it be? You, me, and our dreams.

I give you the gift of a warm cup of tea, so that you may warm your lips, and return that warmth to me—with a kiss.

Heaven.

COMING HOME

On warm summer nights,
when the prairie floors are
flooded by blue shadows of
moonlight, the fireflies come
out to play, filling the darkness
with hope and candlelight.

The wholesome scent
of wild sagebrush wafts
through the air, curling
itself up in the corners of your
mind like a character from a fable.
But do not worry yourself, love,

there are no lessons to be had here—

other than the first sip
of something sweet should
remind you of red velvet
sunrises come autumn.
The kind of sunrises
you can fold your love into,

to keep you warm,
like a soft blanket come winter.

And of the spring?

COMING HOME

In spring, I return—
to the prairie—
to you.

So, if you can read this—
I love you.

LOUIE

I watch my old dog,
my beagle,
my boy,
my Louie.

He's seen so many years,
all with me,
me with him—
in this house and in this yard,
in my arms and in my heart,
my beagle,
my boy,
my Louie.

He's spent countless hours sniffing
on this, that, and the other.

He's played—
chasing birds,
chasing squirrels,
and chasing cats—
befriending only one.
He has warmed my heart
for seventeen years,
and we both know an end will come,
but not for the love I feel—

LOUIE

for my beagle,
for my boy,
for my Louie.

TRINKETS AND DOODADS

I have a vast collection
of trinkets and doodads—
yes, doodads.

Objects made of stone,
and steel, and plastic,
and wood.

Some old.
Some new
Some—I haven't got a clue.

My ownership is limited
by the length of my life,
not the purpose of it.

My dream was to have someone
special, like you, to share them with,
and to create that which can be
more special than either of us,
and to the truly special, leave
every last trinket and doodad—
yes, doodad.

COUNTRY GIRL

Met a country girl,
many years ago.
She had skin that
looked like copper

laced with gold,
and eyes that
whispered one word:
hello.

I was frozen.
More than spellbound.
Less than aware.
Thoroughly speechless.

Thirty-six years later, I still lose my breath.
Thirty-six years of love and marriage.
Thirty-six years—
spellbound with my country girl.

FADED DREAMS

you were my best friend.
someone dependable,
someone i could trust.

you knew everything
there was to know about me—
and i thought i knew you too.

i thought i knew you,
but i didn't know myself—

and i know how that sounds—
like hammered horseshit,

but i drifted out of touch.

i drifted out of touch
from the whole damn world,
and i drifted out of touch
from you. from my friend.

and i'm not sure how i should feel,
but i know i feel better than i have
in a long while, although i still
don't know this new me very well.

FADED DREAMS

but, let me be honest with you,
just this one time—

clear thinking has long since passed me by,
and not even i really want me around.

how could i dream so much?
how could i?

THE END IS NIGH

I told you the end was coming.
Why do you never believe me?

Sometimes I think everyone sees it but you.

You sit in this house,
afraid of the world—
afraid of everything in it,
except this house.

Look out the window—
the weeds grow green,
next will be the grass.

Before you know it, roses
daisies, petunias, lilies,
spiraeas, and more will grow.

Winter's end is near—
I tell you.

THE OLD MAN AND THE TREE

The old man sits, still as a tree,
watching leaves as they blow by,
he feels the wind, and longs to be free.

Leaves swirl as if waves on the sea,
soothing inner emotion, as
the old man sits, still as a tree.

When leaf lands in hand, he can see
lifelines of another being.
He longs to be one with the wind, and free.

Palms of hand and leaf agree
on the meaning of their lives as
the old man sits—still as a tree.

Dust gathers and circles the tree.
Red maple remains stable
and feels the wind, longing to be free.

Whirligigs ride on winds, to the sea.
The old man longs to fly along,
but he still sits, still as a tree—
he feels the wind, and longs to be free.

MODERN DRAGON SLAYERS

Workers painted business ends
of cheap shovels gold—
    for pageantry.
Men and women in suits wore
clean hard hats and jammed
    the clean, golden
digging instruments against
a mound of crumbled earth.
    Posing for pictures—
    like conquerors,
    like kings and queens—

like kings and queens
descending on the remains of
    a previously slain dragon.
The beast, recently slain by noble knights,
though, not of Camelot,
yet it was they, the kings and queens
    in clean hardhats,
    with their golden spears of
unbreakable steel, with their shiny
    helmets guarding their
    unshakeable will,
claiming to have slain a faux dragon
bested by their noble knights.
    Pathetic.

DARK MATTER OF TIME

Time is conceptual—
created by currents, surging noiselessly,
thundering through metallic veins.

We have been gnawing at its essence
for centuries—
clawing at its gears in hopes that we
are remembered.

Dark matter is theoretical—
a cold, abundant force with invisible
fingers, only seen through imagination.

Thinking we can see dark matter
because we see that which is
luminous, is like thinking
we can see time through clocks.

Luminous matter from shattered stars
created life, or so we believe. But
what if dark matter created time?
What if dark measures light—
measures life?

Or, better yet,
what if dark matter were lost time?

DARK MATTER OF TIME

Like the time you lost closing your
eyes for that one special kiss—
you didn't see it.

All that's left is the sweetest of memories,
an aftertaste, lost in the dark matter of time.

WAITING FOR TOMORROW

I travel, from one dream to the next,
searching for tomorrow—

a land where the sun shines,
until it doesn't, and when it
doesn't, clouds in the sky
well up. They begin to rumble,
and they begin to cry.

But what if tomorrow, in and
of itself, were just a dream;
a myth, created by lunatics—
mad men, whose eyes
perused the sky of the night?

When light poured over the valley
of their now, they trusted their eyes,
as men often do. But moonlight
is merely a reflection, cast by
the sun, captured by the moon.

There is no tomorrow.

STORM

A storm is building inside me.
    No lightning.
    No thunder.
    No rain.

My heart and mind want to run from it,
    but I can no longer
hide behind dark clouds of doubt
    that exploit my apathy
and pacify my emotion . . . I can
    no longer live inside
a lie. Can no longer live . . . like this.

And as for the fakest of friends who
    so boldly said I should run—
hide my truest self from the world.
    Suggesting suppression showed strength.
    Suggesting I should hide behind my eyes.
To them now, I ask:
    Run from what?
    Hide from what?
Run and hide from what?

I AM THE STORM!

I FORGOT YOU

I forgot why you left.
Be it because of—
or despite—me.
I forgot you.

I forgot who you were.
Were you one who cared,
or just another naysayer?
I forgot you.

Of all the people in all
the lands around our
tilted globe, you alone
claim to know me.

Why is that?
Who are you?

I have befriended before—
loved from my first breath.
Not all love is romantic.
Not all love is about you.

Maybe I forgot who you were
because of why you left. Maybe
I circled the globe in my dreams
in search of a new tilt on life.

I FORGOT YOU

Whoever you are, and whatever
you meant remains unclear.
I wonder why that is.
I wonder who you are.

SILVER BULLET

It's fourteen past two—
a.m. that is.
I have been writing for hours,
and the hours have been kind
enough to provide me with words.

Words I wrestle with.
Words that wrestle back.
Words that want.
Words make me want more words.

Rubbing and scratching sounds
outside my studio pull me from
my words. A scratch follows
a rub from the north, and
rub leads to scratch, south.

Security camera shows nothing,
so I open the door to peek out—
still nothing. But still there is
rubbing, still there is scratching.

Flashlight in hand—
courage in heart,
I leap out, and
into darkness.

SILVER BULLET

No werewolf here,
just the stray kitty who
visits me for dinner, weekly.
That cat, silver, with white feet.

What conquers a werewolf?
A silver bullet.
What color is my kitty?
Silver.

Kitty, I knight thee,
Silver Bullet—
nickname, Bullet.
Who's a good kitty?

STUDIO

Stone brown over brick red
over polycarbonate panels,
over my little piece of heaven—
on earth.

I gutted the greenhouse that
once brought me joy—
in truth, it still does.

I added insulation and lighting,
creating a space to create—
a space to think and be.

Grow lights still start pre-spring seedlings.
Seedlings I can speak to—
with voice, and pen, and paper.

Can you hear me seedling?
Are you thirsty?
Do you dream?
I hope so.

I hope you dream of the sun,
and I hope you dream of the moon,
here in my studio,
where we can both grow.

WHEN I THINK OF OKLAHOMA

moon slips,
to the right—
to silky-dark, shadowless skies.

magnolia trees,
white flowers, glossy leaves—
reflect lost moonlight from behind canvassed skies.

salt flats,
beyond grassy hills and bottomless valleys—
conceal soft crystals beneath sky mirrored sand.

and finally, sunrise,
golden-yellowish-orange—
sand color changes, though only in our minds.

VOODOO DOLL

I am going to fetch myself a voodoo doll—
of myself, to punish he who needs it most.

Lie once, the doll gets poked—once.
One hateful remark and the doll gets it twice.
Any loss of courage, the doll will cease to be.

And what of good for the doll—from me?

Truth given is praise given, and a new shirt.
Compliments given others, a new hat, perhaps.
Courage could land my doll new shoes—maybe.

And the gift I most wish to give my doll?

Whenever I descend into crowds of humans,
the doll will enjoy the safety of my pocket,
where I often wish I could go at such times.

WANTS AND DREAMS

Good morning world.
I wish I was ready for you—
ready for your excitement,
ready for your energy,
for your light,
ready—
for you.

But how do I make ready
when everything within
my home feels so right—
right under my covers.
I want to stay.
I want to sleep.
I want to dream.

That's why I spent yesterday
packing dreams into boxes.

Boxes of books, stacked
one atop another, line
the east end of my bedroom—
where the sun rises.

WANTS AND DREAMS

Boxes of broken wine glasses
and shattered yesterdays
line the west wall—
where the sun sets.

It is here that I dream—
between unforgotten yesterdays
and today's endless possibilities.
How I wish I could dream longer.

But my life,
much like my home,
needs cleaning—
today.

SEE ME

As the sun rises over a world I used to know,
I begin sifting through the debris,
looking for yesterday,
and what was.

A muffled crunch announces itself from within
the silence, deliberate in its approach,
like a feral cat—
hunting.

Intent and unafraid, I continue searching for
fragments of myself in the wreckage,
sifting through images of strangers
wearing masks, pretending
to be my friends.

They think I can be something I am not,
but I refuse to be who they want me to be.

And as for you—

I remember you called me imperfect—
a human trainwreck—
a pariah.

Well, I am not yours to label—
not yours to define.

SEE ME

You dislike me because I will not be a puppet.
You dislike me because my eyes are open—
wide open—
and I see you.

See me.

HERE COMES ANOTHER

I tried to fit in.
I tried, and I tried, and I tried.

But, even as a child, I was different—
except in my dreams

My buck teeth and freckled face
made me quite the catch in Fairyland.

There, nobody cared that I was German,
and nobody cared that I was Mexican.
In Fairyland, none of that mattered.

But when I became older and wiser—
I foolishly chose to abandon Fairyland.

Harsh reality immediately set in as I realized,
some among us never see beyond skin color,
and others believe ethnicity makes us different.

To them I say, I carry my mother's skin color
the very same way I carry my father's name—
with pride.

So, yes—
I am Mexican.

And yes—
I am German.

My skin is white,
My name is Tom.

Tom is who I am.

MYRIAD BOTANICAL GARDENS (OKC)

Took a little time today to wander about
in the heat and humidity of the indoor
botanical gardens, to get a glimpse of life.

Sycamore figs, pineapples and bananas
growing within my hand's reach. Tons
of trees, bushes, cacao and cacti,
and a row of colorful bromeliads—
those left me breathless.

Try to imagine rows upon colorful rows
of bromeliads—orange, red, and yellow,
even pink—
or was that just a paler shade of red?

I nuzzled my face up to a philodendron
leaf, without touching it, mind you.
The massive, beautiful leaf could have
engulfed my ugly face—twice.

My immediate thought: it should have.
It's what I have always wanted—
a mask beautiful enough for others to see.
And happily enough, not noticing me.

DARK BITES

Walking through the wood,
something's moving behind me.
Something's stalking me.
It knows I am alone—
in the dark.

Wind muffles its panting—
muzzles its anger—
for now.
But I am not safe.

Anxiousness bubbles up
from my esophageal track,
tainting my taste,
acrid and revolting—
revoltingly acrid.

A mass moves and closes distance—
distance between the dark and me.

I gather my courage and clench my fists—

pivoting on ball, then heal of foot—

spinning around to face my stalker.

The mass is a pack with many eyes.

Remembering I said I would rather
die in conflict than on my back—
I smile, then charge.

Remember me.

BEHIND ENEMY LINES

I'd begun to think
I was over it—
but it wasn't over me,
or at least that's my best guess.

Sensing hostility,
I pulled the brim of my
ball cap down to insulate
myself from eye contact.

Navigating the stairs,
I spotted a friendly face
and gave her a tap atop
the shoulder in passing.

I treated her smile as a brief
respite and continued to avoid
the inhabitants of this mostly
malevolent territory with caution.

Within seconds of the tap and smile,
my groundward gaze was interrupted
by the most kindhearted "hello" I'd
heard since arriving the day prior,

and I began to believe
not everyone viewed me
as a threat or a stranger,
so I let my guard down.

There, trapped behind enemy lines
with a friend, I located and harnessed
the energy of my smile. There, behind
enemy lines, I was no longer alone.

ADDICTION ANALYSIS

I fell off,
again.
I hurt the ones I love,
again.
I didn't mean to—
but I did.

I could have stopped myself—
but I didn't do that.
I could have refocused my energy—
I didn't do that.
I could have reached out for help—
I didn't do that either.

So, now what?
Shame?
Again?
Meaningless apologies?
Again?

No.

This time, forgiveness is out of reach.
This time, the only way to make things
right is to make changes.

It is time to change *me*.
It is time to embrace a better me.
Watch me work!

INSOMNIA

My mind opens.
Onto the beach, I run.
Running from the ocean—
the land's mass is nearly
as cool as that of water.

I run more—
until water dries,
and grass grows.

No need stopping—
I continued my run,
to hot, hard land.
A land of soil-crusted rock
where I stopped running—

and took a sip of warm tap water.

My feet stand still
in the remnants of an old
castle, or fortress.
Its walls collapsed ages ago.
Its stones were taken in darkness,
to structures built elsewhere,
and there, assembled in light.
Light that still shines—
on and in these walls.

INSOMNIA

Walls held together
by moss and by magic,
by yon wizard.

Was that someone at the door?
Who cares?

My feet are sliding
over the stone topping
of a long walkover bridge.
More concerned of
screaming than of sliding,
I fall off the side,
into ice and water.

Mother nature calls me.
Loudly.

It's awfully cold and rainy
outside the opening of this cave.
This all seemed like a good idea,
at the base of the hill where
we joked the cave looked
as if it could house a dragon.
We ran this way, you and me.
We ran, face-to-rain,
to slay the dragon and—

This warm tap water is actually quite tasty.

INSOMNIA

My horse and I—
we have been riding for days.
We just passed through
the eroded stone gardens
of the final staging point.
Next stop—
Fairyland.

27

Strange how emotions drive us mad, huh?
I guess what I'm trying to say is:
I loved you, and I believed your lies.

To be clear:
I am not trying to speak truth to power,
I am merely comparing fabrication to emotion.

You see, my admiration and adoration for you is far past any sort of aesthetic appreciation for the amusement you feel as I slip into a fit of rage and anger. And I know my anxiety piques your curiosity, but your displays of awe over the boldness of others have brought about feelings of awkwardness, not boredom. Boredom is that place where salient servings of calmness and confusion lead one to craving anything other than disgust.

As for empathic pain, it is not tonic for understanding, it is entrancement that displaces excitement due to fear. Due to the horror I feel as others imagine me having interest in their joy.

I mean, joy? Really?

Now there's a thought that evokes a sense of nostalgia. It's akin to admitting relief, knowing full well that romance and sadness are one and the same.

As for the satisfaction we feel when we dive head-first into a pool of sexual desire; well, that should come as no surprise.

BROWN HEADED BLACKBIRDS

You greedy little bandits!
Yes, I filled them.
Yes, you're welcome to them.
But share a little, huh?

A swarm of black and brown
amassed on my lawn and in
my trees. Flew in from
the east with the rising sun—

to my freshly filled feeders.

Feeders, emptied in less
than a day. What am I
supposed to do when red,
blue, and grey come to play?

You greedy little bandits!

REBIRTH OF THE AMERICAN (BISON)

Brown and black masses charge across the painted prairie floor in a frenzied celebration of life. The land shutters. A scattering of trees in the distance shakes from constant pounding of hooves.

One hoof after the next threatens to shatter the ground beneath it as dirt and grass become glowing mirrors of reflection and doubt.

Time has come when hunter's greed has swollen their heads like over-ripe pumpkins on the verge of splitting. Bullets roar like thunder and splinter the very fabric of the natural world around them.

From the ashes, formerly known as morality, our people have finally seen enough of this madness and a cessation of the violence is announced. The near extermination of a people has been rivaled only by the near extermination of a species. Somewhere along the way, we've found it within ourselves to just—be.

Masses of brown and black now serve as a reminder of strength and of mercy, and of the difference we can make.

SEASONAL

spring in the air
speaks of pollen.

summer in the sun
speaks of heat.

autumn is the color
we all fall for,

until old man winter
breathes again.

so, we plant,
and we grow,
and we harvest,
and we know—

one season,
is as beautiful as the other,
and the other—
even more so.

even more so.

FINDING MYSELF

Rush of recoil clings to scent of cordite,
scent of cordite clings to freedoms other
Americans take for granted, while I
continue to pay their price—
every damn day.

And every damn day I force myself to wake—
I force myself to rise, and to be. I find myself
feeling the weight of regret on my breath—
not because of the price I paid, but
because of my own pitiful lack of candor.

Because I feel like I never became
who I was meant to be, and because
I'm ok with that.
I like this lie—
because I miss the rush of recoil.

I MISS MY ARMY FRIENDS

We were nothing—
nothing if not tough.
Rough & Tough—
Lean & Mean—
we were far more than nothing.

We were friends,
not just buddies.
Smoking & Drinking—
Running & Hiding
from anyone not our friend,
and from love—
especially from love.

If we fell in love, what would become of our friends?
What would they do without us?
And who would we become?

In the end we did,
we all fell in love.
some kept in touch—
some, not so much.
We were far more than nothing.

SOVEREIGNTY

Pundits, or rather, fools,
tell us mankind is earth's gift.

They view our species
as conquerors and caregivers,
as thinkers and communicators.

To these foolish pundits I ask:
Why, then, do we destroy so much?
Why do we crave money?
Why wealth?
For greed or power?

Money is a manmade unit of measure
designed to share commodities through trade.
It is, by design, benign.

Wealth skews conceptions of money,
distorting commodities' purpose.

Greed tightens malicious ropes
of power around our necks—
power that was never ours.

TRIGGER WARNING

Crisis Line comes from a very real, very dark place. I wrote it as a sort of coping mechanism, the day after I called the Veteran's Crisis line (in crisis). It has graphic thoughts of hopelessness and centers around a veteran who is contemplating self-harm. The Veteran in the poem finds new hope through the Crisis Line Representative who answers his cry for help (he refers to her as Angel).

I use him and her because I was him, and my angel was a female voice on the other side of the line.

To be absolutely clear, this poem was not written for those people in crisis, and I would recommend that anyone in crisis call the angels of the Crisis Lines that are available 24/7.

DEDICATION

This poem (Crisis Line) is dedicated to the compassionate people who work Crisis Lines (veteran or otherwise). Lives are saved on a daily basis, and I believe we can save even more lives if we can only remove the stigma that surrounds the very thought of calling.

To be absolutely clear (again), this poem was not written for those people in crisis, and I would recommend that anyone in crisis call the angels of the Crisis Lines that are available 24/7.

To my angel(s): you are more important than you can ever imagine. People do not want to be in crisis and are often unaware they are in need of help until the time is upon them. Thank you so much for your kindness and thank you so much for saving my life.

CRISIS LINE

Friend—
I can nearly taste you.
Twelve-gauge,
pump-action—
full of lead-based
buckshot, and propellant.
Please take me from my pain!

My god, who am I?
Maybe I should challenge the
cowardly bastards who challenged me,
but I am well past weary—
and I too have cowardice.
That is why I wield the false hope
of a twelve-gauge shotgun,
knowing that "I" am the weapon,
and I am also my worst enemy—

until I hear the voice of an angel,
answering my anguish from
the other side of a distant, digital line.

My crisis was your challenge—
and your challenge was met with
both kindness and compassion.

CRISIS LINE

I needed you more than I told you,
and I needed you, more than
you could possibly know.

My life lay in your hands, Angel.
My duty, my honor, my respect.
Like a lone, dark samurai,
I am nothing without my honor,
and I would have been nothing
if not for you—Angel.

I wonder how many brave
veterans have fallen, before me—
their trembling fingers gripping
cold instruments, ill-suited
for feelings, emotions, or whatever
the hell it is that I'm feeling—
RIGHT NOW.
***

Cliché, I know, but to the angel
on my shoulder that I never knew
existed, you saved me from myself,
and you are so much more than cliché.

You are the voice of reason, carried
triumphantly over newly seen
soundwaves of digital distance.

I will never forget you—
my angel.

About a Few of These Poems

TEARS OF RAIN

My granddaughter gave birth to my great-granddaughter during the COVID pandemic. While it's impossible for me to know how much the whole ordeal affected my granddaughter, I do know how much it affected me. I really did walk out on the porch, and I really did see a firefly descending from my sycamore tree—that beautiful little bug really inspired me to write this poem. I couldn't settle on stanza or prose, so I gave it a bit of both.

FAIRY RING

I planted a circular garden (one circle within another circle) to make my great-granddaughter her very own fairy ring/fairy circle. Her imagination when playing in the yard is all the payment an old man ever needed to know he did the right thing.

CIRCLE AT MIDNIGHT

Taken as a continuation of Fairy Ring, this poem was written before we actually enacted it. We gathered around the fairy circle during the first full moon of spring (pink moon), and we followed this poem to the letter. We then used flashlights to show mineral deposits and saw glowing specks and acknowledged the return of our beautiful fairies.

About a Few of These Poems

GREY HAT

A silly little poem written about a silly little girl. We took a picture of my great-granddaughter wearing my grey hat. The hat was kind of big on her but looked so much better on her than me. I wrote a poem from the picture.

AS I SLEEP

I was depressed and thought about all of the times I had wanted to tell someone I loved them, and for some unknown reason, never did. I used this as a catalyst for a sad love poem on the subject.

TEARDROP

Nothing to see here but a love poem written for my wife after I realized that I'd been manic for quite some time. I don't know what lands I traveled to, but I do know that my mind was not where I was for a very long time.

SUN FOUR

I found information about The Aztec Five Suns myth on the internet. In one version, the fourth sun began crying and continued to do so for 52 years. I used the image my mind made about a young man being washed out in the rain. The father figure at the end was blind but was also a seer. I saw this as the elderly seer passing the baton to a younger, sighted seer.

STORYTELLER

Storyteller is an interesting poem that can get a little confusing. It was taken from a book of fiction I've been working on. Basically, a banshee has taken a woman hostage and is berating her in unspeakable ways (as I imagine a banshee would). The banshee refers to her

About a Few of These Poems

captive as Fae because "Fae" always wanted to be a fairy. Anyway, I need to get around to finishing that book.

CIRCLE OF LIFE

This poem is a staggered glimpse of what an apocalypse might look like, from the inside, in real time. I used the over-mining of magnetic materials as a sort of catalyst for the poem (that's why magnetic north shifted).

COMING HOME

As a soldier in the United States Army, I had the pleasure of being stationed in South Korea three times (12 months each). During my first two stints, the lack of modern technology limited communication between my wife and me. This poem is about those times, before the third tour when high-speed internet brought us free video chats.

LOUIE

I am constantly sad or crying watching Louie struggling a little to make it to his seventeenth birthday. He is in such a good mood, and he is so sweet—and, of course, I love him so much. Louie was born on 17 May 2008.

DARK MATTER OF TIME

Ok, this poem was super fun to write. I was watching some documentaries on dark matter and got this crazy image in my mind about how dark matter could be lost time and I just ran with it. I threw in the kiss at the end for what I believed to be a beautiful and powerful image that spoke directly to the premise of the poem.

About a Few of These Poems

THE OLD MAN AND THE TREE

This was my very first villanelle. I wrote it after visiting an area near Norman, Oklahoma. I was holding a very large blackjack oak leaf in my hand and enjoying a conversation with my brother-in-law when I began comparing the leaf's lines to the lines in the palm of my hand. I wondered if there was a lifeline and which line that might be, then started writing a poem about a half-hour later. Anyway, after it sat around doing nothing for a couple of years, I decided to selectively deconstruct some of the villanelle out of it—just to give it a personal touch.

WAITING FOR TOMORROW

Waiting for Tomorrow was originally named I Travel (using the title line as the first line of the poem). When I decided to name this collection after its premise, I renamed it. There are a few poems in this collection that make reference to tomorrow as being more of a concept than a reality.

STORM

Yes, storm is an angry poem. Yes, I am the storm. Storm was started as a poem that would just kind of describe my personal anger issues, but it sat in my hard drive for a couple of years waiting to be finished. I really got it finished when I was thrust back into the world of being an artillery instructor because I thought a person in the IT industry with a BA in English could find work elsewhere. I was wrong, I was upset, and I just let it loose. Oh, it used to have some bad language in it, but I edited that part out.

SILVER BULLET

Bullet is what I named one of the stray cats that came by to visit me weekly while I was laid off from work this last winter—the other's

About a Few of These Poems

name is Mustache (he's black with a white chest and face, and he has a black mustache).

BEHIND ENEMY LINES

Ever walk into a building and feel like you weren't wanted, much less liked? Well, that happened to me lately. Not because of perception but because of reality. To the two dear friends that saved me from my own thoughts of inadequacy, thank you so very much.

27

I was reading that there are now 27 categories of emotion. This satirical poem addresses all 27 categories in alphabetical order. It is spoken though the lips of a person who is being abandoned by a love interest, and that person is making use of a salty attitude to convey their message.

REBIRTH OF THE AMERICAN (BISON)

Some people may think this poem is about Native Americans while others will opine it is about the American Bison. Both are in the poem, but they are not what the poem is about.

There are countless species on the verge of extinction, and we have proven long ago that we have it within ourselves to save them. THAT is what the poem is about. Be the change.

CRISIS LINE

As stated in the trigger warning and dedication, this poem comes from a very real, very dark place. I wanted this collection to be full of poetry that spoke of me, my family, and my life. Obviously, this is something I have problems sharing, but I wanted an honest collection. Also, still being honest, I did not go as far as the narrator of the poem did, but I did reach out and I did get the help I needed—from my own guardian angel that I never knew existed.

www.ingramcontent.com/pod-product-compliance
Lightning Source LLC
Chambersburg PA
CBHW071732040426
42446CB00011B/2322